MUHAMMAD OF MECCA

MUHAMMAD OF MECCA

Prophet of Islam
by Elsa Marston

A Book Report Biography
FRANKLIN WATTS
A Division of Grolier Publishing
New York / London / Hong Kong / Sydney
Danbury, Connecticut

JB
Muhammad
M

ACKNOWLEDGMENTS

The author gratefully acknowledges the assistance of Dr. Salih Altoma and Dr. Scott Alexander of Indiana University; and in Beirut, Lebanon, of Dr. Hisham Nashabi, Makassed Association, and Dr. Ahmed Moussalli, and Dr. Nadim Naimi, American University of Beirut.

Maps by XNR Productions

Cover photograph ©: SuperStock.

Photographs ©: Art Resource, NY: 29 (Foto Marburg), 19, 71 (Giraudon), 101 (Erich Lessing), 92 (Scala); Bridgeman Art Library International Ltd., London/New York: 108 (BAL58105, Ar5847, Celebration of the End of Ramadan, from "The Maqamat," (The Meetings) illustrated by Hariri, second quarter thirteenth century, Bibliotheque Nationale, Paris), 54 (BAL28563, MS447, view of Medina and mosque of the Prophet Muhammad, Ottoman, eighteenth century, Chester Beatty Library and Gallery of Oriental Art, Dublin); Christine Osborne Pictures/MEP: 103; Corbis-Bettmann: 9 (Archivo Iconográfico, S.A.), 95 (Richard T. Nowitz), 67, 75, 84, 87; Mary Evans Picture Library: 39, 57, 78; North Wind Picture Archives: 14, 21, 47, 88; Stock Montage, Inc.: 59, 63; Stone: 44 (Bill Aron), 2 (Nabeel Turner); The Art Archive: 52; TRIP Photo Library: 115 (M. Jelliffe), 8, 27; Wolfgang Käehler: 82.

Visit Franklin Watts on the Internet at:
http://publishing.grolier.com

Library of Congress Cataloging-in-Publication Data

Marston, Elsa.
 Muhammad of Mecca : prophet of Islam / by Elsa Marston.
 p. cm.—(A book report biography)
 Includes bibliographical references and index.
 ISBN 0-531-20386-7 (lib. bdg.)   0-531-15554-4 (pbk.)
 1. Muòammad, Prophet, d. 632—Juvenile literature. 2. Muslims—Saudi Arabia—Biography—Juvenile literature. [1. Muòammad, Prophet, d. 632. 2. Prophets.] I. Title. II. Series.

BP75 .M34 2001
297.6'3—dc21   00-042641

GROLIER
PUBLISHING 1 2 3 4 5 6 7 8 9 10 R 10 09 08 07 06 05 04 03 02 01

3065200092 4482

CONTENTS

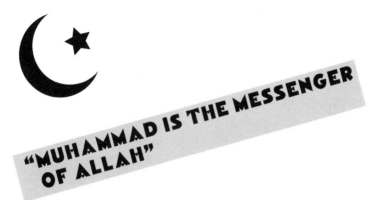

"MUHAMMAD IS THE MESSENGER OF ALLAH"

La ilaha illa Allah . . . Muhammad rasul Allah. "There is no god but Allah. Muhammad is the messenger of Allah." This statement, in Arabic, is the basic creed of every follower of the religion known as Islam. Today, more than a billion people believe in the faith taught by the Prophet Muhammad.

Muslims have revered Muhammad since the days of his mission on Earth. But just who was Muhammad? A ruler, a saint, a great thinker? Is he a legendary figure—or was he a real man?

Muhammad was a real man—a historical person who lived in the western part of the Arabian Peninsula in the late sixth and early seventh centuries. Since he lived more recently than the founders of other major religions, we have more information about his life. From the time he started preaching, Muhammad was in the public eye. His followers remembered things he said and did,

Pilgrims at the Ka'ba in Mecca

and these sayings and actions were preserved in writing.

Over the centuries, thousands of biographies of Muhammad have been written. Most have a religious viewpoint, setting forth the quality of Muhammad's life for devotional purposes. Other accounts, written by Europeans in the past, took a negative view, because many Europeans saw Islam as the enemy of Christianity. Recently, some non-Muslim scholars have attempted to present Muhammad's life story objectively, in a historical way.

How can we look at Muhammad as accurately as possible, trying to be free from all bias? What sources provide factual accounts of this man's life?

First, while a great deal has been written about Muhammad in the past, we do not know

A NOTE ON THE KORAN

The word *Koran* can be spelled in different ways, such as *Qur'an*, which is closer to the correct sound in Arabic. *Koran* is used in this book because it is more familiar to non-Arabic readers. The Koran is divided into 114 chapters, or *suras*. They are arranged in order of length, starting with the longest and ending with the shortest. Each sura is divided into verses.

There are many English translations of the Koran. The translation used for verses quoted in this book is *Al-Qur'an: A Contemporary Translation* by Ahmed Ali (Princeton University Press, 1988). It includes Arabic and English text and was chosen for ease of locating verses, readable format, and comprehensible language.

An early Koran written on parchment

how much is accurate. Even detailed records may be faulty or may reflect the writer's personal views. They can also get changed over time. With a figure as revered as Muhammad, there was a tendency to exaggerate or even make up stories to illustrate his extraordinary qualities. Also, the first attempts to write the story of his life came a hundred years after his death or more. Much of our information, therefore, has to be understood as religiously inspired, rather than as historical fact.

A number of sources do exist. The most important is the holy book of Islam, the Koran, which consists of the revelations that Muhammad believed came to him from God. The Koran contains references to events in Muhammad's life.

However, the Koran does not present events in chronological order. Muhammad received many revelations at different times and then recited them to his followers. The followers preserved the revelations partly in writing but largely by memory, since that was the custom of the time. About twenty years after Muhammad's death, the revelations were gathered together. One of Muhammad's successors appointed a group of people to compile the revelations into one large collection following an arrangement said to have been specified by Muhammad. Since that arrangement did not follow the order in which Muhammad had spoken the revelations, the Koran does not read as a historical narrative.

In addition to the Koran, we have reports of Muhammad's sayings and actions by people who said they had been there and were eyewitnesses. These are called the *hadith,* which means "speeches" or "reports." Many people claimed to have witnessed Muhammad's actions, and a huge collection of *hadith* accumulated after his death. Islamic historians in the seventh and eighth centuries tried to determine which were authentic and which were not. Using the *hadith* judged most reliable, plus the Koran, Islamic historians then wrote detailed accounts of Muhammad's life. Those histories are the third major source of information available to scholars today.

This biography is based on the information that most scholars today, Muslim and non-Muslim, believe can be accepted as reasonably accurate. It aims to introduce the story of Muhammad to non-Muslim readers, while providing helpful and interesting information for Muslim readers. It is the story of an extraordinary man who realized his unique calling and accomplished his goals, with great and lasting benefit for the spiritual development and civilization of humankind.

CHAPTER ONE

THE EARLY YEARS

The young mother proudly named her first son Muhammad, "the praised one." But while rejoicing, Amina must have grieved, because the child's father would never see his son, nor would the child know his father. Muhammad's father, a merchant, had died on a caravan trip a few months earlier.

The year was A.D. 570, and the place was Mecca, a town in the western part of the Arabian Peninsula, inland but not far from the Red Sea. The people of Mecca and the region around it were Arabs and spoke Arabic, a Semitic language that has changed relatively little since that time.

For a while, Muhammad and his mother lived with his paternal grandfather, who was the head of the clan of Hashim, one of the important families in Mecca. When Muhammad was one or two years old, his mother, following a local custom, sent him to live for a few years with a nomadic

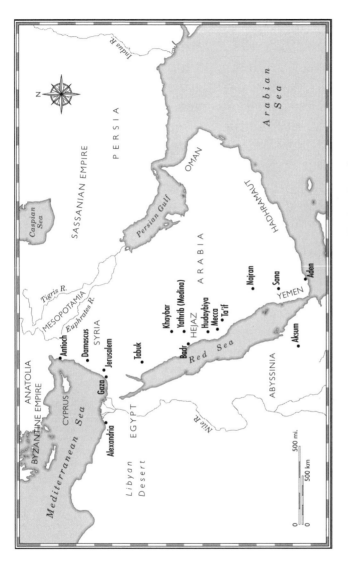

Arabia at the time of Muhammad's birth, about 570

desert tribe. The women of Mecca believed that the desert air was healthier than the air in the town and that the rough life of the nomads, called bedouin, would strengthen their children. In return, the bedouin women received gifts and help from the city families.

Little is known about Muhammad's childhood, but stories told after his death reveal popular beliefs about him. According to one story, Muhammad's mother, a widow with no money, at first could not find a bedouin woman willing to care for her little boy. Finally, Halima, a woman of one of the poorest tribes, accepted the child. Hali-

A bedouin camp in the Arabian Desert

ma had no milk for her own child, her camels' milk had dried up, and even her donkey was sick. But when she took Muhammad into her care, her own milk flowed, her camels produced great quantities of milk, and her donkey outran all the others.

Another story tells of a day when little Muhammad and one of Halima's children were playing outside the camp. Suddenly the bedouin boy came rushing to his mother in terror. She went with him and found Muhammad lying on the ground. When he could speak, he told her that two men in white had suddenly appeared. They had taken his heart from his body, washed it clean in a bowl of snow, and replaced it in his body, purified. Then, blessing him, the angelic creatures told him of his future greatness, and vanished.

A YOUNG ORPHAN

Not long after Muhammad returned to Mecca, his mother died. Two years later, his grandfather died. Fortunately, the young orphan, still only about seven or eight, was taken in by an uncle. Abu Talib, who was now the head of the clan, treated the boy kindly. But as he had a large family to support, and his clan's fortunes were declining, Abu Talib could not provide Muhammad with schooling nor a hopeful future. Muhammad probably helped tend his uncle's camel herd, and later went with Abu Talib on trading journeys.

Popular stories tell us that even in his youth Muhammad showed signs of future greatness. It is said that once when Muhammad accompanied his uncle's trade caravan to Syria, they were invited to stop for a meal with a Christian monk who previously had ignored

The mark of prophecy

the caravans. This time he noticed a small cloud following the caravan as if shading someone special from the sun. He looked over his guests, then asked if there was anyone else in their party. The caravan leaders brought in Muhammad, who had been left outside with the camels. After questioning him, the monk examined the boy's back and discovered a certain mark. Declaring it to be the mark of prophecy, he urged Muhammad's uncle to take care of the boy, for a great future lay ahead of him.

We can imagine that Muhammad was a thoughtful, serious youth. Born into a good family but soon orphaned, brought up by his uncle but without resources to build a future, he may have reflected soberly about his prospects. And that may have made him more aware of the society around him.

MECCA, MUHAMMAD'S HOME

Mecca, where settlements had existed since ancient times, appears to have been a busy town in the latter part of the sixth century. The land was hilly and the soil too poor for agriculture, but the town's location had advantages. Situated at a natural stopping place for caravans, with adequate springs, Mecca became a trading center.

Caravan routes came to Mecca from the Persian Gulf and Mesopotamia (now Iraq) in the east, from the rich lands of Yemen in the south, and from wealthy cities to the north, such as Damascus and Gaza. Traders brought expensive goods from distant places, such as silks and spices from India and China. The Meccan merchants carried these goods to other cities and brought back food and other luxury items in exchange. Two large caravans left Mecca each year, for Syria in summer and Yemen in winter.

Some of the tribes that had formerly been nomadic were now settling in Mecca to make money. The town was growing.

Trade was not the only reason for Mecca's prosperity, however. For centuries, Mecca had been the most important religious center in the region. Although some towns had Jewish and Christian communities, most people in Arabia followed pagan religions. These religions involved worship of many different deities, such as forces in nature represented by stones and figurines.

In the center of Mecca, a sacred open space surrounded an ancient shrine: a square building with an unusual black stone embedded in one corner. This building was—and still is—called the Ka'ba. People considered it to be the shrine of a high god known as "the god," or in Arabic, "Allah."

In addition to Allah, the "Lord of the Ka'ba," there were many other gods. Idols of 360 lesser deities stood in the sacred area. Twice a year, people came on pilgrimage to this religious center from all over the Arabian Peninsula. The pilgrimages meant a great deal to the desert tribes.

"Lord of the Ka'ba"

Worshipers performed rituals at the Ka'ba. They "circumambulated" the building, that is, walked around the outside, and visited other shrines in Mecca and nearby. Times of pilgrimage were "holy months," periods of peace when no fighting was allowed among the tribes. At all times, the area within a 20-mile (32-km) radius of the Ka'ba was considered sacred ground, where violence was prohibited. People came to Mecca from near and far to rest from the rigors of daily life and the stress of tribal warfare.

A busy trade fair took place at the time of pilgrimage. The bedouin sold food and wool products

A painting from a ninth-century Koran shows the city of Mecca, set amid the mountains.

from their flocks, the townspeople probably sold manufactured items to the bedouin, and traders sold luxury goods. Supervision of the religious shrines and sacred wells, plus all the buying and selling at the fair, produced wealth for the upper classes of Meccans, especially those families who had gained control over the holy places.

TRIBAL CULTURE

Although Mecca was a thriving town, it was still tied to the traditional tribal culture of Arabia. Tribes were groupings of many families related by blood and descended, they believed, from a common ancestor. The society of Mecca reflected some important aspects of tribal culture.

In the Arabian Desert, people could not survive except as part of a group. Everyone had to belong to a tribe. The nomadic tribes valued their independent way of life, free of control by outsiders and emphasizing strength, endurance, and the ability to survive under harsh conditions. But because those conditions were so harsh, especially in times of scanty rainfall and scarce food, the desert tribes lived in constant competition. They fought for the necessities of life—water, forage for their animals, food, and territory. Warfare and raiding went on all the time—except, of course, during the "holy months."

In this uneasy life, the tribe looked after each person and supported any of its members who were in need. It also defended any member who had trouble with outsiders, regardless of who was at fault. In return, tribal members put the tribe's interests and welfare ahead of their own. Each tribe had a chief, or a group of chieftains, whose decisions were supported without question.

Another important individual in tribal culture was the poet. Middle Eastern peoples have always loved poetry. In Arab culture—the culture of the Arabian Peninsula and all Arabic-speaking countries—the spoken word has great power. It can arouse intense emotion—delight, passion, sorrow, or anger.

Poets were the tribes' promoters. They recited long poems praising their own tribes and insulting enemy tribes. This was not simply art or entertainment. Poems were serious political statements, which shaped public opinion. When poets directed their verses against an enemy,

A poet recites the glories of the tribe.

their words were thought to possess an almost magical force.

The tribal way of life offered advantages. In a tribe, each person was protected by the chief. No one could be hurt or killed without severe consequences—because the tribe would seek revenge. A person who did *not* have the protection of a tribe, however, could be killed or persecuted and no one would take much notice. The tribal leaders supported widows and orphans—of which there were many, because of the constant fighting. A strict code of justice and a generosity of sorts regulated welfare within the tribe.

When tribes settled down to urban life, much of the tribal system and way of thinking lingered. People were still known by their tribe, or, more often, by their clan within the tribe. Tribes still looked after and protected their people. By the seventh century, however, the traditional tribal system was starting to fail. New social classes, leaders, and bonds of loyalty were appearing. Business alliances were becoming more important than traditional clan obligations.

As the merchants competed to gain riches and power, they thought more of their own wants and accomplishments than of the tribal group's needs. Successful people grew proud, feeling no longer bound by traditional social customs. They neglected their responsibilities toward the less fortunate. Needy people, including the many widows and orphans, received little help or were deprived of resources that were rightfully theirs. The poets now sang the praises of the rich, their new patrons.

Muhammad must have become aware of these problems and been distressed by the breakdown in social responsibility. As a poor young man, however, there was little he could do.

MUHAMMAD'S YOUTH

As he grew to manhood, Muhammad became known for his good sense, reliability, and honesty. He was called *Al Amin*—"the trustworthy." Around 590, he evidently took part in an alliance of several clans, which aimed to defend the oppressed and promote fair trade practices.

A story illustrates Muhammad's good reputation. When the Ka'ba shrine needed repairs, men from several clans worked on it together so that no single clan could take credit. After rebuilding the walls, they had to replace the sacred black stone. They quarreled over which clan would have that honor. When Muhammad arrived to make his circumambulations, the men turned to him for a solution. He told them to spread a cloak, place the stone in the center and, with a representative from each clan holding the edges of the cloak, lift it together until the stone could be fitted in place. Muhammad's ability to find peaceful solutions appeared many times in his later career.

In his mid-twenties, Muhammad evidently went on trading expeditions to Syria. A Meccan widow named Khadijah, who had inherited her husband's wealth and thriving business, had hired Muhammad to make a trading journey to Syria as her agent. What she observed of him so pleased her that she proposed marriage and Muhammad accepted. The only way he could acquire the means to start his own trading business was through marriage to a wealthy woman.

This was no self-serving marriage on Muhammad's part. He cared for Khadijah deeply and was devoted to her throughout their long marriage of around twenty-five years. She was an equally loving wife. Although older than Muhammad, she bore him six children. Their four daughters lived to maturity, but the two boys died in infancy.

From the age of twenty-five, Muhammad enjoyed the life of a moderately prosperous trader. Although he could afford to live well, he continued his frugal ways, giving away much of his income to the poor. Whatever she may have thought of this, Khadijah was always loyal. The emotional support she provided Muhammad proved all-important when his life took an astonishing turn.

CHAPTER TWO

THE FIRST REVELATIONS

Near Mecca, the countryside rises into barren, rocky hills. In his middle years, Muhammad often escaped the bustle of the town by going to a certain cave in these hills. Like other Meccans, he may have occasionally taken his wife Khadijah and their children along on a family retreat, but usually he went alone. It was not simply peace and fresh air that Muhammad sought, however. Always a thoughtful person, he probably prayed and meditated, seeking spiritual guidance and pondering questions about the meaning of life and about humankind's relationship to God.

THE FIRST COMMAND

One day, when Muhammad was about forty, he had an experience that totally changed his life. Suddenly, as he was praying in the cave, he saw an overwhelming radiance. From this intense light, he heard the command "Recite!" Amazed, he protested, "I cannot recite."

"Recite!" But the command, which now appeared to come from an angel who filled the sky, was repeated. The angel called Muhammad the "Messenger of God" and told him to "Arise and warn."

This was the way Muhammad later described the experience. He was terrified and even feared that he might be losing his mind. What did the command "Recite" mean? *What* should he recite? He hurried home to Khadijah, who helped him through the shock of his experience and then urged him to talk with her cousin, a man named Waraqah.

Waraqah was one of the few people in Mecca who had converted to Christianity. Hearing Muhammad's description of his vision, Waraqah said it was like the experience of earlier prophets, particularly Moses. Waraqah's words reassured Muhammad and helped him accept the role of messenger that appeared to have been thrust upon him.

Over the next two or three years, Muhammad returned to the cave and received further messages, or revelations. He did not yet make public the message he believed God wanted him to convey, but told only his close family and friends.

This period of quiet was probably a time of reflection, occasional doubt, and growing conviction.

THE MESSAGE

At this time, Muhammad had no thought of starting a "new" religion. His mission, he believed, was to restore the people of Mecca to the true faith in one God, founded some 2,500 years earlier by

The rocky landscape outside Mecca offered solitude. Today, visitors come to see a cave believed to be the one in which Muhammad meditated.

Abraham, the ancient patriarch of Jewish and, later, Christian tradition. Muhammad wanted to revive that faith. God, he believed, had chosen him to bring the Meccans back from their sinful ways and beliefs in pagan deities, and lead them into a correct relationship with the one God.

The most important part of Muhammad's message, therefore, was belief in the one, all-powerful God. In Arabic the word

Allah, "the God"

for God is _Allah_, literally, _al-Ilah_, meaning "the God." Muhammad was not talking about a new and different god for a new and different faith. He was talking about the same God worshiped by the Jews and Christians.

Muhammad emphasized God's goodness and mercy. As creator of the universe, he said, God provided humans with everything they needed. In return, human beings must acknowledge God's supreme power and show their gratitude for God's goodness by prayer and by good acts.

Sometime after death, Muhammad's message revealed, everyone would face a Judgment Day. God would reward or punish each individual according to whether his or her life had been good or wicked. If people acted selfishly or with cruelty, they would have to account for their actions before God.

Muhammad also emphasized his role as God's

messenger, the last and most significant in the long line of prophets since very ancient days. Henceforth, he was known as the Prophet.

These beliefs provided the basis of the religion that came to be known as Islam. The word

A fourteenth-century Muslim manuscript includes a painting of God's angels.

Islam is related to the word for "peace," but its specific meaning in this case is "submission." Islam means submission to the will of God and God's plan for the world—a submission that will

_____

"One who submits"

_____

bring perfect peace. A Muslim—"one who submits"—is a person who has accepted this belief. Muslims are also called "believers." Although scholars are not sure when the term Islam was first used, it appears that after a few years Muhammad's followers were said to believe in Islam and call themselves Muslims.

THE KORAN

As Muhammad preached, listeners memorized what he said and some may have kept written records. He, too, memorized the revelations and repeated them in worship. In this way, the early revelations were preserved. Later, Muhammad's messages were recorded by a scribe. The collection of revelations eventually came to be known as the *Koran*, which means the "reading" or "recitation." The Koran became the holy book of Islam.

Muhammad believed that the revelations in the Koran came from God, usually through an angel, and Muslims hold to this belief. In other words, they believe that Muhammad did not think up the ideas in the revelations, and did not "write" the holy book. He carried the messages from God to the people. Revelations came to him throughout his life, often at times of stress when he needed guidance. Those who witnessed him receiving a revelation said he went into a trance-like state.

The command that Muhammad heard in the first vision—"Recite!"—is often interpreted as "Read!" and his reply as "I cannot read." Some people argue that Muhammad's reply meant that he was illiterate. If this is true, they reason, he could not have known the biblical information that some revelations contain—so the information must have come from God. Scholars have no clear knowledge of whether Muhammad was literate; but he lived in a society where people learned by recitation, and he could have learned the biblical material in other ways than by reading.

RELIGIOUS INFLUENCES ON MUHAMMAD

At this time, Muhammad must have been influenced by ideas and beliefs from various sources. These influences may have helped prepare him to receive the visions and revelations.

According to Islamic tradition, for many years Muhammad had believed in one deity or god (monotheism), rather than in the existence of multiple gods (polytheism). He identified the one, all-powerful God as Lord of the Ka'ba—Allah. Muhammad was not the only one who believed this. The idea of one God was growing among other thoughtful people in Mecca.

Whether or not he could read the biblical scriptures, Muhammad almost certainly knew something about the beliefs of Judaism and Christianity, including stories from the Bible. During his travels as a merchant, he probably met Jews and Christians. The cities of Syria and Palestine, some of which he may have visited, were then Christian, part of the Christian Byzantine Empire ruled from Constantinople. Certain Arab tribes in the northern part of Arabia had adopted Christianity, and some Christian monks lived in the desert. Muhammad also knew converted Christians in Mecca, such as his wife's relative, Waraqah.

Some cities had Jewish populations, and large, powerful Jewish tribes had lived in Arabia for years. Scholars are not sure whether these tribes were people who had migrated from Palestine or Arabs who had converted to Judaism.

Many people in Mecca knew that the Jews and Christians both had holy books, the biblical scriptures, to help unify them and guide them in their religion. The pagan Arabs had nothing like that. Muhammad might have felt that having a holy book would be of value to his people.

The troubles of his society also probably filled

Muhammad's thoughts. He was unhappy with the rivalry among the clans in Mecca—while the *good* values of tribal society, such as help for the less fortunate, seemed to be fading. Many of the merchants concerned themselves only with their own power and possessions, and the ordinary people were losing their sense of security. A thoughtful person like Muhammad might have concluded that his people needed a new kind of community, with a new set of values, to guide them. With these concerns on his mind, Muhammad must have been ready for a spiritual experience.

Before long he decided to tell others the important truths that he believed had been revealed to him, whatever the cost. For two or three years, Muhammad shared the revelations only with those close to him. When he felt ready to preach to the people of Mecca, he had fifty followers. Who were those people, and what drew them to Muhammad?

THE FIRST MUSLIMS

Khadijah was his first follower, for she immediately supported him and believed in his message. Two young men, actually boys, were the first male followers: 'Ali, the cousin of Muhammad, and Zayd, a youth in Muhammad's household. Later, both played important roles in the history of

Islam. Abu Bakr, a merchant and good friend of Muhammad's, was the first man of relatively high social standing to accept Muhammad's message. He was a loyal "right-hand man" throughout the Prophet's career.

Some women besides Khadijah followed Muhammad, but most of the early converts were men. Young men were attracted by the Prophet's message, perhaps because they were more open-minded and sensitive to the problems of their society than were the members of the older, self-satisfied generation. Some of the first believers came from prominent clans in the city, but probably more came from the lower classes. These included slaves and people without clan ties. Those who accepted Muhammad's message early and remained close to him throughout his life are called the Companions.

The Companions

The ordinary people of the city listened sympathetically, even if they did not flock to join him. Many had suffered from the selfish actions of the wealthy merchant class and were probably glad to hear that behavior condemned.

Other reasons why people listened to Muhammad's message can easily be found. Pagan religion contained little that was spiritually uplifting or had intellectual appeal. In contrast, monotheistic religion, with roots in biblical tradition, offered spiritual meaning and guidance. Islam was an inclusive faith, a religion for *all* people regardless of tribe or class. Its promise of reward for virtuous living also attracted people.

Not least of all, Muhammad doubtless spoke with eloquence and held people's attention with his quiet but forceful personality and his strong character. He is said to have had the ability to win both loyalty and affection.

FIRST OPPOSITION

Not everyone, however, was glad to hear what the Prophet had to say. His message was bound to upset Meccan society.

The largest and most powerful tribe in Mecca was the Quraysh. Many clans—including Muhammad's own clan, the Hashim—belonged to this tribe. The Quraysh dominated trade, controlled the holy sites, and reaped profits from the annual pilgrimages. Because of their power and arrogance, the Quraysh became the target of Muhammad's criticisms, and they quickly took the lead in opposing him. In fact, historians often call Muhammad's adversaries simply "the Quraysh."

At the start of his mission, Muhammad was a respected member of society. But that situation soon changed. When Muhammad had gone to see his wife's Christian relative Waraqah, after receiving the first revelations, Waraqah had mentioned a warning found in the Bible: a prophet is despised among his own people. The truth of that warning, echoed in the Koran, now became clear.

We [God] *never sent an admonisher* [warner] *to a town but its well-to-do people said: "We do not believe in what you have brought." And further: "We have far more wealth and children than you, and we are not the ones to be punished."* (Sura 34, verse 34)

At first the rich merchants ignored the Prophet. As his criticisms grew sharper, merchants assumed he was seeking wealth and power. They tried to buy him off with promises of riches, power, and prestige. He rejected every offer, saying his mission had nothing to do with these things.

For a while the Quraysh believed Muhammad's message meant that Allah, the Lord of the Ka'ba, was first among all the deities. They could accept that. But when Muhammad denounced all the idols of the pagan religion, the Quraysh rose up in anger. They said his messages came from an evil spirit, or from some secret adviser, probably a foreigner. Maybe he was possessed or mad, they suggested. They insulted and ridiculed Muhammad and his followers, saying that the low social class of many of his believers proved the foolishness of his message.

The Quraysh mocked the idea that all humans would face God's final judgment after death. How, they asked, could bodies rise up after they had decayed to bones? And if Muhammad was really God's messenger, he should perform a miracle. After all, they argued, God ought to send an angel as messenger, or at least an important person—certainly not just an ordinary merchant.

Muhammad steadfastly repeated that he claimed no supernatural powers. His role was to preach the truth and warn his people of the results of wrongdoing. The Koran, he said, was the only miracle involved in his mission.

REASONS FOR OPPOSITION

Although Muhammad did not speak against pilgrimages, the Quraysh merchants may have worried that if the idols were destroyed, pilgrims would stop coming to Mecca. Then their profits from the pilgrimages and fairs would drop. The fear of economic losses may have been one cause for their opposition to Muhammad's preaching.

They seem to have been even more concerned about the Prophet's challenge to their business practices, social power, and way of life. They did not want to hear about a "Judgment Day" at which their worldly wealth would not help them. They were stung by Muhammad's attacks on their greedy behavior. More-

All persons are equal before God

over, when Muhammad said that all persons are equal before God, it sounded like a threat to their place in society. They could see that his message appealed to the common people, which fueled their fears about his political ambitions. If he became strong enough, he might be dangerous.

Not least of all, the Quraysh could not bear to see their ancestors' beliefs overthrown. Arabian society was conservative. Even though the Meccans had plenty of material goods, in their thinking they were still close to the harsh life of the desert. People who live in constant fear of hardship tend to hold on to "old ways" rather than take risks with new ideas. Many people of Mecca, therefore, felt it was best to hold on to the faiths of their ancestors—the age-old worship of idols.

When you ask them to follow what God has revealed, they say: No. We shall follow what we found our ancestors following." (Sura 31, verse 21)

A pilgrimage to the Ka'ba has been an Arab tradition since before Muhammad's time. This diagram of the shrine is from a sixteenth-century Persian pilgrim-book.

THE SATANIC VERSES

A puzzling incident occurred a few years after Muhammad started preaching. One revelation he received seemed to say that people could worship at the shrines of three important female deities, and that would be acceptable to God. When Muhammad made this revelation public, it was understood as a compromise with the Quraysh.

Then Muhammad received another revelation, which denied the earlier one. No, this message said, the three deities had no special standing and, like all other idols, must be rejected. Muhammad explained that the first message could not have come from God, but must have come from Satan. Therefore the false revelation came to be called the "Satanic verses."

After this event, the Quraysh stepped up their attacks. Muhammad and his followers from powerful clans were safe from physical attacks, because their clans would avenge any violence against them. They were publicly insulted, however, and on one occasion the pious Abu Bakr was dragged around by his beard. Some believers who had defied their families by following Muhammad were locked up in their houses. Some followers without clan support were beaten, or tortured by being exposed all day to the intense sun.

The persecution became so intense that in

615 Muhammad advised a group of his followers to leave Mecca and cross the Red Sea to Abyssinia (now Ethiopia). The king of Abyssinia, a Christian, was known to be a humane man. He granted the refugees asylum and protected them even when a Quraysh delegation demanded that he hand them over. Some of the refugees returned to Mecca after a few years, but little is known about the fate of the others.

As their next move, the Quraysh began an economic boycott of Muhammad's clan. No one was allowed to do business or make marriage arrangements with them. Apparently the boycott was not enforced strictly enough to cause real hardship, however, and it was dropped after two years.

LOSS OF SOME VITAL SUPPORT

Then in 619 a double blow—truly disastrous—struck Muhammad. First, his beloved wife Khadijah died. This loss was soon followed by the death of Muhammad's uncle, the head of his clan.

Abu Talib's death had important effects. Abu Talib was never a believer because he was unwilling to give up the traditional religion of his ancestors. Yet he honored his tribal obligations and protected Muhammad from the Quraysh attacks.

The new head of the Hashim clan, Abu Lahab, was a different sort of man. Abu Lahab had opposed Muhammad for some time and had joined the Quraysh alliance against him. Possibly looking for an excuse to withdraw the clan's protection, he asked the Prophet whether their grandfather, the former chief of the clan, was now in hell. Muhammad had to reply that this was true, for according to the message he preached, any pagan who had not accepted Islam must be in hell. Abu Lahab used this answer as a reason to banish Muhammad from the clan.

Now Muhammad was vulnerable. Without clan protection he could no longer preach in Mecca, and his life might be in danger. To find some other source of protection, he journeyed to a town called Ta'if, high in the hills about 40 miles (64 km) from Mecca. His hope that the clans there would help him, however, was quickly shattered. The people of Ta'if believed strongly in their pagan idols, and their leaders were in league with wealthy Meccan families who had summer homes in Ta'if. They rejected Muhammad's request and encouraged the local rabble to throw stones at him as he left the town.

A story, drawn from a Koran verse, tells of Muhammad's despair as he left Ta'if. Taking refuge in an orchard, he felt that there was no hope except in God. Soon someone came to him, the servant of a man who had taken pity on him. The servant, a young Christian slave, gave

Muhammad fruit and listened to him intently. The Prophet took this kindness as God's way of answering his prayers. He resolved to return to Mecca.

From outside the city he sent messages to the heads of other clans, requesting protection. The third one he contacted agreed to be his protector. With that assurance, he entered Mecca. However, he found matters no better. His enemies grew more aggressive, and his followers faced hostile abuse.

At this time, probably the darkest days of his mission, Muhammad apparently had an extraordinary spiritual experience. One night, after reciting the Koran at the Ka'ba, he fell asleep beside the shrine. In his sleep he saw the angel Gabriel, who placed him on a pure white horse and took him on a miraculous flight through the night to Jerusalem. There they alighted at the Temple Mount, where they met Abraham, Moses, Jesus, and other prophets. Muhammad was offered a drink for refreshment—water, milk, or wine. His choice of milk meant symbolically that Islam should be neither too strict nor too worldly and luxury-loving. Then Muhammad and Gabriel ascended to heaven, climbing a ladder that rose through seven heavens to the Throne of God.

This spiritual experience must have reassured the Prophet. Yet the outlook for his mission was discouraging . . . until an offer of help came his way, from an unexpected source.

Muslims have venerated Jerusalem since the time of Muhammad. This mosque, the Dome of the Rock, has foundations dating from the seventh century.

CHAPTER THREE

THE BREAK

In spite of the hostility he faced, Muhammad continued his mission of preaching to anyone who would listen. Sometimes he was able to talk with pilgrims who came to worship at the Ka'ba.

THE APPROACH FROM YATHRIB

In the summer of 620, Muhammad met six pilgrims from a settlement called Yathrib, 250 miles (402 km) north of Mecca. They were so impressed by the Prophet and his message that they returned the next year in a group of twelve, representing all the major clans in Yathrib. This group promised to accept Muhammad as the prophet of God and follow the rules of virtuous living that he explained. When they returned to their homes, Muhammad sent one of his trusted followers with them to instruct the people about

Islam—and perhaps to keep him informed about conditions in Yathrib.

This effort bore fruit. The next year, a party of 75 Muslims came from Yathrib for the pilgrimage. Meeting Muhammad secretly, they made a significant promise. They confirmed their loyalty and, if necessary, they would protect the Prophet by force of arms.

Why were these few pilgrims from Yathrib ready to help a man seen as a dangerous troublemaker in Mecca? Because Yathrib itself was in trouble, and this move seemed a good way out.

Unlike Mecca, Yathrib was not a clearly defined city. Instead, it was the most densely populated center in an oasis of about 20 square miles (51 sq km). Although surrounded by barren terrain, the land of the oasis was heavily cultivated, mostly with date palms and grains. The people lived mainly from agriculture, not commerce.

But like Mecca, Yathrib was going through social and political changes, partly due to the recent settling of nomadic tribes. The traditional practice of raiding among tribes had worked in the desert, but it did not work in settled communities. The clans of Yathrib, constantly fighting among themselves, had become so hostile and suspicious of one another that they could not resolve their differences. No single party was strong enough to impose its will, and no leader could be trusted to act fairly.

Then the pilgrims met Muhammad in Mecca.

Yathrib was located in an oasis—a fertile area with water in the midst of a desert region.

Wise and neutral, he seemed the answer to their prayers. They hoped he could bring peace to Yathrib through his powerful personality, his sense of fairness, and his stature as a prophet.

There was a second reason why Muhammad appeared to be the "man of the hour." Among the many groups living in Yathrib were three large tribes of Jews, plus some smaller Jewish communities. How they happened to settle in this oasis is not clear, but they were an important part of the society—skilled and prosperous farmers, craftsmen, and merchants.

"Man of the hour"

They lived like the Arabs, except that they were better educated and had a strong sense of their religious identity.

From these Jewish tribes, the people of Yathrib already knew something about Jewish religion. Belief in one God was an idea familiar to them. They had also heard the Jews speak of an expected messiah. When Muhammad presented himself as God's final prophet, with a new God-given holy book, it was not hard for the people of Yathrib to believe that he was the promised savior. They had better lay claim to him, they may have thought, before the Jews did! For practical, political, and ideological reasons, therefore, the leaders of Yathrib were glad to have Muhammad come to their community.

At the same time, they knew that the Quraysh regarded Muhammad as an enemy. The Quraysh would consider his move to Yathrib a defiance of traditional tribal loyalty. This was a serious matter, which could lead to hostilities. By offering a new base to the Prophet, therefore, Yathrib might invite attack . . . and Mecca was much stronger. Thus the actions of the people of Yathrib could have grave consequences.

THE EMIGRATION

Muhammad sought shelter in Yathrib for himself and for any followers who accompanied him.

Their departure from Mecca is called in Arabic *hijrah,* meaning "emigration"—a separation from one's family and attachment to a new community.

In the summer of 622, small groups of Muslims began to leave their homes in Mecca and make the ten-day journey by camel to Yathrib. They left quietly, to avoid arousing suspicions. Either the Quraysh were slow to realize what was happening, or they were glad to be rid of troublesome people, because it appears that little was done to stop them. Muhammad stayed till the last, to encourage any who might waver. No one, however, was forced to make the move, and some Muslims stayed on in Mecca.

Finally, of the seventy or more who intended to leave, only Muhammad, Abu Bakr, and 'Ali were left in Mecca. By now, according to the traditional story of the Prophet's life, Muhammad was aware that the Quraysh leaders knew of his plan and had made one of their own: they intended to assassinate him. To avoid bringing blood-guilt on any one clan, a group of young men from all the major clans would attack the Prophet together. Having learned of the plot, Muhammad escaped from his house by a back window. His brave young cousin 'Ali disguised himself as Muhammad and took his place. By the time the would-be assassins discovered that the person on Muhammad's bed was not the Prophet but 'Ali, Muhammad was safely away. 'Ali, too, escaped.

Nonetheless, Muhammad was still in danger. Beyond the city limits he was outside any clan's protection. Traveling with Abu Bakr, he hid in a cave near Mecca for three days and then followed a little-traveled, roundabout route.

A traditional account of Muhammad's departure from Mecca says that while he and Abu Bakr were hiding in the cave, a search party passed in front of the entrance. Miraculously, an acacia tree had sprung up in front of it overnight, and a spider had spun a web across the cave opening. A dove had built a nest on a rock and was sitting right where a person would have to climb in order to reach the cave. So the pursuers, certain that no one could be inside the cave, passed on. Muhammad and Abu Bakr waited a while and then, being careful not to disturb the dove, climbed out and resumed their journey on two camels that had been hidden nearby.

In September, Muhammad and Abu Bakr reached a settlement in the southern part of the oasis of Yathrib. A few days later, the Prophet moved to a more central part of the oasis. To avoid arousing jealousy by choosing land belonging to one particular group, the Prophet said he would make his home wherever his camel stopped. The good camel did indeed kneel on an appropriate bit of land. Muhammad bought the property and, with his followers, set to work to build a house. This building included a large courtyard for meetings and worship. In time it became the first mosque—an Islamic house of worship.

Two significant changes in Islamic history occurred now. Yathrib became known as Medina. Its full name, *Medina al-Nabi,* means "the City of the Prophet." The town has been called Medina ever since.

"The City of the Prophet"

More important was the adoption of a new basis for reckoning time. The Islamic era dates from the time of the *hijrah* (July 622), and uses the letters A.H., for *Anno Hegirae,* meaning "the year of the Hijrah," or "After Hijrah." The Islamic year consists of lunar months—six months of 29 days each and six of 30 days each—making a yearly total of 354 days rather than 365. Therefore, the Islamic calendar does not coincide exactly with the calendar used in the West. For example, the year A.D. 2000 is the year 1421 A.H.

These changes demonstrate what a radical move the Emigration was. The Muslims from Mecca left their homes, families, and also their religious center—the most sacred place in Islam, the Ka'ba. This shrine, to which the pagan Arabs had been so devoted, was now the shrine of God. None of the Muslims knew whether they would ever return to this place of such spiritual importance to them.

A miniature painting shows early Muslims building Muhammad's mosque in Medina.

They were also breaking all ties with their own clans and accepting the protection of a distant tribe with which they had no blood relationship. Since blood ties were the foundation of their society, this act was painful for the Muslims and offensive to their original tribe, the Quraysh of

Mecca. Many must have wondered how their Prophet could see them through the days ahead.

FIRST YEARS AT MEDINA

In Medina, Muhammad faced new challenges. He was no longer an ill-treated prophet, preaching to a small group of followers. Now he would be the founder and director of an entirely new type of community. He had not pursued a political role in Mecca—but now he evidently felt that God wanted him to assume political leadership.

At first, Muhammad was like the head of a minor clan, not as important as the established tribal chiefs of Medina. Nonetheless, he had a special status, and quickly came to an agreement with the Medinans that made his power clear.

That agreement was a written covenant known as the "Constitution of Medina." It declared that the Muslims from Mecca and the Medinans— Muslims and Jews—would live in harmony, with loyalty to Muhammad and no treacherous dealings with the Muslims' enemies. They would become a single united community called an *umma*, distinct from all others. Tribal loyalties now took second place. The Islamic *umma* could be described as a super-tribe that brought together people of all tribes. It was a grouping based on belief rather than on kinship.

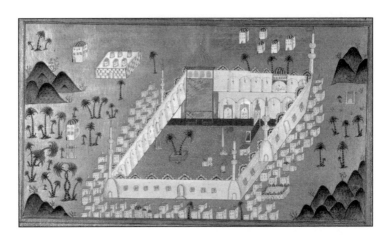

An eighteenth-century painting shows Medina and the mosque of the Prophet Muhammad.

The agreement spelled out relationships and duties. The most striking provision was this: "Wherever there is anything about which you differ, it is to be referred to God and Muhammad." God was thus the supreme authority, while Muhammad, although in most respects a clan chief like any other, was God's agent in settling disputes.

The two groups of Muslims, those from Mecca and the residents of Medina, used different names. Meccans were called the Emigrants, while Medinans were the Helpers or Supporters. It appears that the majority of the Medinans, aside from the Jews, accepted Islam at this time.

Not every Medinan, however, was delighted with an arrangement that gave an outsider so much power. Thus a third group came to be recognized: Medinan Muslims who said they accepted Islam but who opposed Muhammad as a political leader. They are referred to as the "Hypocrites," or "Doubters"—meaning people who say they believe something but are not really sincere. Their loyalty was questionable at times of conflict. The Koran contains many criticisms of the Hypocrites, who must have annoyed Muhammad a good deal.

> *When asked to desist from spreading corruption in the land they say, "Why, we are reformers." Yet they are surely mischief-mongers. . . . When they meet the faithful they say, "We believe"; but when they are alone with the devils their fellows, they say: "We are really with you; we were joking."*
> (Sura 2, verses 11-12, 14)

MUHAMMAD AND THE JEWISH CLANS

Having some knowledge of Judaism, Muhammad assumed that the Jews of Medina would welcome his preaching. He emphasized Islam's roots in the monotheistic faith founded by Abraham, hoping that this would appeal to the Jews. His aim was to reveal the pure truth of Abraham's religion, stripped of errors that had crept in over time. If the Jews did not actually become Muslims, he thought, at least they would be loyal supporters.

At first many of the Jews listened to Muhammad. Some taught him more about the scriptures and their religion, particularly the role of Abraham. Muhammad learned that the Jews of Medina considered the Ka'ba to be Abraham's shrine, built by the Patriarch and his oldest son Ishmael as the first temple of God in Arabia. This meant that the Arabs, too, through Ishmael, were descendants of Abraham. What greater proof could be needed, Muhammad must have reasoned, that the religion he taught was the original faith founded by Abraham?

Muhammad adopted several Jewish practices to show Islam's closeness to Judaism. Religious fasting and the choice of Friday for the weekly worship were both related to Jewish custom. Most important, he followed the Jewish practice of praying while facing toward Jerusalem, the holy city of Jews, Christians, and now Muslims.

The call to prayer was another practice similar to one followed by the Jews. Jewish custom was to blow on a ram's horn. Muhammad decided that a *muezzin,* or crier, would mount a high place and sing the call to prayer in a loud voice, five times in every twenty-four hours. Muhammad chose as the first *muezzin* a black African named Bilal. Originally an Abyssinian Christian, Bilal had been a slave in Mecca and had become one of Muhammad's early Companions. During the persecution by the Quraysh, he was staked out in the hot sun all day with heavy stones on his chest. His faith never wavered—and his voice remained strong as well.

By preaching, by argument, and by adopting some of their ways, Muhammad sought to win over the Jews. Yet they rejected him. Firm in their own beliefs, they saw no reason to accept him as the ultimate prophet, much less the messiah promised by their scriptures. Another factor was that in the tribal rivalries, the Jewish tribes were losing

In a nineteenth-century picture, a muezzin issues the call to prayer from the minaret of a mosque.

power. This newcomer from Mecca was a threat who could make things worse. While a few Jews remained friendly, many began to criticize and ridicule Muhammad. The growing split between Muhammad and the Jews pained and angered the Prophet. Soon it would lead to hostility.

A sign of the break came abruptly, in the second year of the *hijrah*. Muhammad received a revelation that told him to change the direction of prayer. No longer would Muslims pray facing toward Jerusalem; instead, they would pray toward the Ka'ba in Mecca. This change emphasized the Arabian roots of Islam.

FOUNDATIONS OF ISLAMIC SOCIETY

Although the Prophet faced conflict during his first months in Medina, he succeeded in getting the Muslim community on a firm footing. Revelations kept coming, providing guidelines for a new way of life based on piety, justice, and fair solutions to everyday matters. There was a change in the nature of the revelations. Those that the Prophet received in Mecca were mostly about the nature of God, submission to his authority, and warnings against wrongdoing. The revelations received in Medina frequently provided rules for society.

O believers, eat what is good of the food We have given you, and be grateful to God. . . .

Forbidden to you are carrion and blood, and the flesh of the swine. . . . If one is obliged by necessity to eat it . . . he is not guilty of sin; for God is forgiving and kind. (Sura 2, verses 172-173)

When any one of you nears death, and he owns goods and chattels, he should bequeath them equitably to his parents and next of kin. (Sura 2, verse 180)

They ask you [Muhammad] *of wine and gambling. Tell them: "There is great enervation* [loss of strength] *though profit* [usefulness] *in them for men; but their enervation is greater than benefit."* (Sura 2, verse 219)

Devout Muslims pray facing Mecca, on a prayer mat to separate the person from the earth.

There is no sin in divorcing your wives . . .
but then provide adequately for them, the
affluent according to their means, the poor
in accordance with theirs as is befitting.
This is surely the duty of those who do good.
(Sura 2, verse 236)

Trade has been sanctioned [permitted]
and usury [taking unfair interest on a loan]
*forbidden by God. (*Sura 2, verse 275)

Ramadan is the month in which the
Qur'an was revealed as guidance to man. . . .
So when you see the new moon you should
fast the whole month; but a person who is ill
or traveling . . . should fast on other days, as
God wishes ease and not hardship for you.
(Sura 2, verse 185)

If a debtor is in want, give him time until
his circumstances improve; but if you forego
the debt as charity, that will be to your
good. . . . (Sura 2, verse 280)

Meanwhile, the Prophet's role expanded from
spiritual guide to leader in all aspects of life. He
became the head of a community that relied on his
authority in economic, social, and political affairs,
as well as religious matters. He proved his states-
manship through his personal qualities of wis-
dom, good judgment, and patience. Before long,
this role began to take on even larger dimensions.

CHAPTER FOUR

MUHAMMAD'S CAMPAIGN

The Muslims were safe in Medina—but Muhammad wanted more than safety. His objective was to return to Mecca in triumph and in peace. In Mecca lay the heart of Islam, the shrine of the Ka'ba, where the Muslims longed to be able to worship freely. First, however, the opposition of the Quraysh would have to be overcome.

To return to Mecca meant preparing for encounters with his enemies. At the time of the Emigration, one revelation to Muhammad signaled a major change. No longer would Muslims have to patiently accept hostile actions, as they had in Mecca. They could now actively resist, taking any actions they thought necessary.

> *Permission to take up arms is granted those who fight because they were oppressed.*
> (Sura 22, verse 39)

Henceforth Muhammad revealed a new and different side of his character.

RAIDS AND HARASSMENT

Muhammad's campaign against the Meccans grew partly out of an urgent problem. How were the Emigrants to survive in Medina? They were merchants and bankers, but Medina was not a trading center and they had no capital to start businesses. They knew nothing about agriculture, and there was no land available anyway. They could not depend on the Helpers' charity forever.

For a solution, Muhammad turned to the old Arabian practice—raiding. Raiding was a rough-and-tumble way of redistributing wealth among tribes—almost like a sport. A group from one tribe would stage a quick hit on another, stealing camels and other animals, occasionally women, and whatever else they could carry off. While raiding provided a release for the aggressive energies of the men, actual fighting was avoided if possible, because killing could lead to blood feuds—a life for a life.

Medina had a good location for cutting off the Meccans' trade with Syria. The targets chosen for the first raids, carried out only by the Emigrant Muslims from Mecca, were the caravans of the Quraysh. Muhammad justified this policy by saying that the Muslims had been ill treated by the Quraysh and had lost their property and livelihood. These expeditions, even though small, would remind the Quraysh that the Muslims were alive—and a growing threat to their prosperity.

Before long, the Medinan Muslims, the Helpers, also became involved. The raids then

A thirteenth-century drawing shows a trade caravan.

changed. From the earlier primary goals of gaining a livelihood and harassing the Meccans, they began developing into *jihad*. *Jihad*, which means "effort," is generally

"Holy war" understood as "holy war." The Muslims thought of it as warfare to protect, defend, and advance the Islamic community. It is the only kind of warfare that Muslims are supposed to undertake.

The concept of *jihad* made warfare a sacred duty. It provided justification for Muslims fighting their own kinsmen in Mecca, and for Medinans fighting Meccans with whom they had no quarrel and might even have business and marriage ties. *Jihad* also changed the traditional way of raiding. In the tribal system, alliances could change. Today's friend and raiding partner could be tomorrow's enemy. If, however, a tribe was attacked under the banner of *jihad* and then adopted Islam, it became part of the *umma*, the Islamic community, and would not be attacked again.

In January 624, Muhammad sent off a small raiding expedition. The men headed for a spot called Nakhlah, where they met a caravan bound for Mecca. Pretending to be pilgrims, they joined the caravan and when the time was right, they attacked the four guards on duty. One guard escaped, two were taken prisoner, and one was killed—the first bloodshed in Muhammad's campaign. That death meant trouble because it took place during the sacred month of pilgrimage, when killing was forbidden.

When the raiding party returned to Medina, there was alarm over the violation. Before long, however, Muhammad received a revelation. It said that while killing during the sacred month was serious, to deny God and drive believers away from the sacred shrine in Mecca was even worse. In other words, the wrongdoing of the Quraysh merited punishment even if that punishment violated the rules of the sacred months.

This reassured the Muslims. The Quraysh saw the matter differently. The killing of that guard, they believed, called for revenge. But before the Meccans could act, Muhammad made the first move.

THE BATTLES OF BADR AND UHUD

Two months after the incident at Nakhlah, Muhammad sent about 300 men to attack a caravan returning from Syria. With 1,000 camels, this caravan was probably the major trading expedition of the year for the Quraysh. Somehow the Meccans learned of the planned attack and sent out a large army. Both forces arrived at a place called Badr, which had several wells. Meanwhile, the caravan escaped and returned to Mecca.

This left the two armies facing each other, perhaps not wanting to fight, but unable to withdraw without disgrace. The Quraysh force was larger, but the Muslim troops had a better position and were closer to the water supply. To make things harder for the Meccans, Muhammad ordered all the wells blocked up except one. Then the battle started.

The outcome was a great victory for the Muslims. They lost fourteen men, while the Meccans lost about seventy, including several important leaders. They also took about seventy prisoners of war. Muhammad established a policy of fair treatment for prisoners at this time—another change from traditional tribal warfare. Throughout his campaigns, only under rare circumstances was a prisoner executed.

The Muslim victory had a great psychological impact. The Quraysh had suffered a severe blow to their pride and to their prestige among the bedouin tribes of the region. They now realized that Muhammad and the Muslims were a real threat. As for the Muslims, the battle at Badr convinced them that God was with them. God had delivered them from the uncertainties and troubles they had long faced.

The second major battle came a year later, in March 625. To avenge their defeat at Badr, the Quraysh sent out a much larger army—said to be 3,000 men, with 200 horses, plus camels for the

An illustrated manuscript shows a battle scene.

other warriors. On reaching the oasis of Medina, they camped near a hill called Uhud. There they found that the Medinans' fields of grain were ready for harvest—handy food for their horses.

Seeing this huge force, the Muslims were undecided. Should they remain in the forts in the center of the oasis, thus forcing the Meccan army to lay siege? Or should they go out to meet the enemy? Muhammad favored staying in the forts, but was persuaded that it would be cowardly not to fight, especially with the Meccan army out stripping the grain fields. The Muslims moved out at night and took a position on the hill of Uhud.

Once the battle was underway, it looked as if the Muslims, although outnumbered, would win. But a group of archers left their positions and started seizing battle spoils. The Meccan army then gained the upper hand. Muhammad was wounded and knocked unconscious, and the cry went up that he had been killed. He recovered soon, however, and the Muslims were able to strengthen their position.

At that point, the Quraysh army turned around and headed back to Mecca! Possibly, thinking the Prophet was dead, they felt that their earlier defeat had been avenged. Also, their losses may have been too heavy for them to continue fighting.

The Battle of Uhud was a draw. The Quraysh failed to defeat the Prophet; the Muslims fought well but took a beating. The battle also affected the Muslims' morale. They wondered whether God really was with them, as they had believed at Badr.

Then a revelation came to the Prophet that helped his followers understand their experience. God, he said, had allowed the beating as punishment for disobedience during the battle, and as a test of their faith. Chastened but reassured, the Muslim forces rallied for a parting shot at the Meccans. In a traditional custom of Arabian warfare, they followed the retreating Meccan army and put up a show of strength. There was no more fighting, however, and the forces returned to their home cities.

THE SIEGE OF MEDINA

Muhammad continued to send raids against the Quraysh caravans, and the Quraysh grew increasingly desperate. Their pride and prosperity demanded that they defeat the Prophet.

In March 627, they made an all-out attempt to break Muhammad's power. With allies from large bedouin tribes, a huge Meccan army set out for Medina. It may have numbered as many as 10,000 men, including 600 horsemen. Meanwhile, Muhammad's forces had grown to about 3,000 fighters. Lacking cavalry, however, this number was no match for the Quraysh army. The Prophet had to find some other defensive strategy.

And he did—a device apparently never before seen in Arabian warfare. Following the suggestion of a Persian convert, who knew this strategy was used in his own country, Muhammad decided to dig a large trench on the side of Medina most open to attack. For six days the Prophet and his people wielded shovels, finishing the trench just in time.

The plan worked. The Meccan army was stunned to encounter the trench. It was too wide and deep for their cavalry to cross, and they were not equipped for a long siege. The grain in the outlying fields had already been harvested, so the horses had little to eat. For about two weeks the Meccans could make only minor assaults, which the Muslims held off, and finally they gave up. The last full-scale campaign by the Quraysh ended with a total of eight men killed.

A second part of the Prophet's strategy against the Quraysh was to deprive them of the support of the bedouin tribes. Normally the bedouin would side with Mecca because of its importance as a religious center. Therefore, Muhammad carried out several raids against the tribes, mainly to impress them with his power. These campaigns broke up some confederations of tribes allied with Mecca, persuaded the tribes not to oppose Muhammad, and sometimes won the bedouin to Islam.

Meanwhile, the Prophet faced conflict inside the oasis of Medina. The Hypocrites were one source of trouble. Before Muhammad came to Medina, one of these men had hoped to become ruler of the oasis, and he especially resented the Prophet. Sometimes he played a friendly role; other times, he withdrew his men from battle at

A cavalryman shooting arrows

critical points. He used every opportunity to criticize. These harassing tactics caused trouble, but
did not present a serious threat.

Muhammad's military campaign demonstrat-
ed radical growth and change in his role as political leader. He had been a quiet, mild man,
spending the first twenty-five years of his adult
life in trade and the next ten as a prophet, peacefully preaching the word of God. Suddenly, in his

fifties, he became a military strategist and warrior. Moreover, it seems as though he stepped into this role with enthusiasm. The way Muhammad

A military strategist and warrior

met a variety of challenges, which called for different abilities and energies, is one of the most fascinating aspects of his life.

THE JEWISH TRIBES

In time, Muhammad's relations with the Jews led to problems. The Prophet had been bitterly disappointed when the Jews did not accept him nor the religion he preached. They sided with his opponents in Medina, and they might, he believed, prove untrustworthy in conflicts with Mecca. He began to see their political power as a danger. It would be safest, Muhammad evidently decided, to have them out of the picture.

There were three large Jewish tribes in Medina. At different times, two were besieged in their fortresses and then forced to leave for other oasis settlements that had Jewish populations. The first tribe left for Syria in 624 after the Battle of Badr, and were allowed to take their money and possessions with them. In the case of the second tribe, Muhammad suspected a plot against him. After a siege, they were forced to give up their weapons and leave. Even so, as accounts describe the event, the members of this tribe made a great show of their departure, piling their camels high with possessions and singing proudly as though leaving in triumph.

The third large Jewish group, however, met a violent end. During the Siege of Medina, according to the traditional account, Muhammad learned that this tribe was planning actions against him. He believed this broke a solemn agreement with him. Determined to teach the tribe—and other possible enemies—a lesson, he called for another siege. When the tribe surrendered, there was no mercy. The men were executed, the women and children sold as slaves.

The destruction of this tribe, in 627, was the only time in his military career that the Prophet ordered punitive bloodshed on a large scale. His fight with the powerful Jewish tribes was not based on religious intolerance but on political concerns; for he believed that the most important thing was to preserve the Islamic community. Smaller Jewish groups who presented no political threat were allowed to remain in Medina and live in peace.

Now the Prophet could be sure that his position in Medina was secure, with no serious opposition or source of betrayal. He was ready for the final stages of his campaign to regain Mecca.

CHAPTER FIVE

THE ROAD BACK TO MECCA

The Quraysh were reeling from the major encounters at Badr, Uhud, and Medina, along with the Muslims' attacks on their caravans. Yet Muhammad evidently did not want to take Mecca by force. It appears that he had a broader vision: the bringing of Islam—and unity—to all the Arab peoples. For this he needed the Meccans to accept him peaceably and to become part of the Islamic community. But how could that happen, when feeling in Mecca still ran so high against him?

THE PILGRIMAGE TO MECCA

Muhammad was a master of the unexpected. In a surprising move, inspired by a dream, he decided to make a pilgrimage to Mecca to worship at the Ka'ba. More than piety lay behind this move, for the pilgrimage would show that Islam was an Arabian religion. In March 628, he left Medina with as many as 1,600 followers. They wore the plain white garments of the pilgrim and brought with them seventy camels. The animals would be killed in a traditional ceremony and their meat given to the poor.

The Meccans got word of the Muslims' approach. Suspicious of Muhammad's intentions, they sent out 200 horsemen. In the hilly country, the Muslims evaded the cavalry and stopped at a place called Hudaybiya, just outside the sacred territory of Mecca. It is said that Muhammad's camel, the same one that had carried him on his *hijrah* to Medina, knelt at that spot and refused to budge—evidently an omen.

A caravan of pilgrims on the road to Mecca, with the leaders carrying aloft the bebak, or standard

Faced with this large group in the hills, the Quraysh did not know what to do. If they denied pilgrims the right to visit the Ka'ba, they would anger the bedouin tribes, who valued the pilgrimage so highly themselves. But if Muhammad entered Mecca, it would be a triumph for him and would make the Quraysh look weaker. Some way out of the predicament had to be found.

THE TREATY OF HUDAYBIYA

As the Quraysh leaders tried to understand Muhammad's motives and assess his strength, a series of messengers and representatives traveled between Mecca and the Prophet's camp at Hudaybiya. Finally Muhammad and the Meccan leaders made a treaty that covered several points.

First, a ten-year truce would begin immediately. Next, the Muslims agreed that they would not enter Mecca that year but could return for the next year's pilgrimage. Also, any Meccan who tried to join Muhammad without clan permission would be sent back, while any Muslim who went over to Mecca would *not* have to be returned. The bedouin tribes could ally with either side.

By negotiating with him, the Quraysh had accepted the Prophet's authority and recognized him as an equal. The provisions of the treaty allowed them to save face, yet guaranteed the Muslims could make the pilgrimage peacefully the next year. The treaty also showed how confident Muhammad was that his followers would never choose the other side. In fact, the treaty gave him just about all he wanted.

But the Prophet's fellow pilgrims were dismayed. To come all that way, and then bow to Quraysh opposition and turn back? They saw the treaty as a defeat.

All Muhammad's skill and shrewdness were required to turn this critical moment into a victory. In a dramatic gesture, he decided to carry out the pilgrimage rituals at Hudaybiya—shaving his head and killing a sacrificial camel. This evidently convinced the believers that he was in control and that their interests and their religion would triumph. To show their loyalty, all the other men followed his example, shaving their heads and killing the sacrificial camels. After that, they returned to Medina.

In 629, as provided by the treaty, about 2,000 men, accompanying the Prophet, set out on the pilgrimage. The Meccans left town and stayed in the hills for three days to avoid trouble. Even so, Muhammad managed to contact the new head of the clan of Hashim, his uncle Abbas, who agreed to accept Islam.

Following the pilgrimage, the Prophet tried to further strengthen his position. He sent out expeditions to win the allegiance of the bedouin tribes, and organized the growing Islamic community. Many individuals and tribes, won over by the Prophet's prestige as well as his religious ideas, were converting to Islam. There is evidence that Muhammad even sent messages to the heads of nearby states—Abyssinia, Egypt, Persia, and the Byzantine Empire. According to popular belief, he urged them to accept Islam. More likely, he was

A nineteenth-century engraving shows the white costumes of male and female pilgrims to Mecca.

trying to reach a political understanding with them.

Among the Quraysh, in contrast, morale was weakening. The leadership was split, and increasing numbers of people considered accepting Islam. Muhammad's strength and piety, along with the remarkable loyalty of his followers, had made a deep impression during the negotiations at Hudaybiya.

Meanwhile, the Treaty of Hudaybiya was falling apart. Tribal quarrels broke out, involving both the Meccans and Medinans. The new leader of the Quraysh, Abu Sufyan, went to Medina to talk with Muhammad personally. Although a strong foe of the Muslims, he was also intelligent and realistic, and by now he could see which way the wind was blowing. It is likely that he came to some understanding with Muhammad about the future of Mecca.

THE MARCH ON MECCA

With increasing numbers of Muslims and tribal followers, plus some high-placed friends inside Mecca, Muhammad was ready. On January 1, 630, he set out, with an army that is said to have numbered about 10,000 men. At a distance from Mecca, the Prophet ordered his army to spread out and light 10,000 campfires, so as to appear even larger and more intimidating.

Seeing this show of strength, Abu Sufyan and some of the other Quraysh leaders came to Muhammad's camp. In return for a promise of general amnesty for the city, to include everyone who stayed at home and did not resist, they gave their allegiance to the Prophet.

Four columns of the Muslim army then entered the city from four directions. With hardly any fighting, Mecca surrendered. A few of the Quraysh leaders were made prisoners, and a small number were executed for actions that

The Prophet's hope Muhammad saw as treason. For the rest of the population, the death of the old regime came peaceably and the new ruler and religion were welcome. That, it appears, had been the Prophet's hope and the goal of his strategy all along.

Muhammad remained in Mecca about two weeks. One of his first orders was to have all the idols in the sanctuary and in private homes destroyed. From that time on, only the Ka'ba, the shrine to Allah, was to be revered.

Having won Mecca, the Prophet went back to Medina, which remained his home for the rest of his life. In the amazingly short period of seven and a half years, he had conceived and carried out his plan with total success. Driven from his native city, he had returned a victor, recognized as God's Messenger. He had made Islam, at first the faith of a small, persecuted minority, the religion of the most sacred center in Arabia—soon the religion of a fast-growing state. And he had started a new religious and social system that would quickly spread for hundreds of miles around.

AFTER THE RETURN TO MECCA

Although the Meccans had been Muhammad's enemies for fifteen years, he was able to gain their support remarkably soon after his return. The appeal of Islam as a religion and a social system won them over, as did Muhammad's policy of amnesty and offers of important posts. Then, too, the Prophet was clearly the new power in the region.

Yet Muhammad still faced opposition and was soon gearing up for battle once more. A large grouping of tribes that had old grievances against the Meccans made a challenge at a place called Hunayn. Muhammad gathered a force of about 12,000 and marched against the tribal army, said to number 20,000. The tribes were so confident of victory that they even brought along their families and possessions.

In terms of numbers, the Battle of Hunayn was the largest in which Muhammad ever took part—but not the fiercest. The Muslims gained a

The desert landscape outside Mecca

decisive victory and a great deal of booty. Wisely, the defeated tribes decided to accept Islam.

A flood of tribal groups now came to offer allegiance to Muhammad. Occasionally rival factions within a tribe competed with each other to be first, and the Prophet was faced with situations that required skillful handling. Not all tribes, however, chose to become Muslim immediately. Muhammad made alliances with those who kept their own religion, imposing payments on them to support the growing Islamic community. The *umma*, in fact, was becoming like a political state.

The Muslims in Medina were well off by now, thanks to the last important campaign Muhammad waged before his march on Mecca. In May

628, he had besieged Khaybar, a rich oasis with a large Jewish population whose leaders had been stirring up neighboring bedouin against Muhammad. When Khaybar surrendered, Muhammad decreed that the people could keep their possessions and land, but must give half of their agricultural produce to the Muslims. This started a practice later used in the expanding Islamic Empire. As groups of Jews and Christians were drawn in, they were required to pay a tax to the Islamic government but allowed to keep their own religion, land, and livelihood.

THE LARGER WORLD

While the Islamic community grew stronger in western Arabia, the politics of the region were changing. Since the sixth century, the Middle East had been under the sway of two "superpowers." In the western part was the Byzantine Empire, a Christian empire with its capital at Constantinople (now Istanbul, Turkey). Its empire stretched from southeastern Europe to North Africa, including the countries along the eastern Mediterranean. Farther east lay the Persian Empire, which included today's countries of Iran, Iraq, and Afghanistan. Among the Persians the main religion was Zoroastrianism, a belief system started by the Persian prophet Zarathusthra who lived about a thousand years earlier.

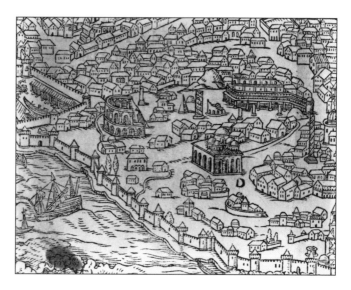

A sixth-century map of Constantinople, capital of the Byzantine Empire, shows the remains of a Roman circus and hippodrome with several obelisks amid the central ruins.

The two empires competed fiercely, first one and then the other dominating the region. Probably because the Arabian Peninsula was mostly desert, inhabited by fierce and unruly tribes, neither empire tried to control it. However, some small, wealthy states along the Persian Gulf and South Arabia were connected with the Persian Empire.

Then, weakened by long years of warfare, the Persian Empire started to crumble. Yemen and other states on the southern edges of the Arabian

Peninsula turned to Muhammad. At the same time, Muhammad evidently arranged with tribes in northern Arabia, near Iraq, to raid that part of the Persian Empire. In this way, the Islamic state started to expand toward both the south and the east.

The Byzantine Empire, in the north, was a greater challenge to the advance of Islam. In 630, Byzantine power was strong. Moreover, the tribes in northern Arabia were mostly Christian. Allied with the Byzantine rulers, they could not be won over to Islam easily.

For some time Muhammad had been sending small expeditions north toward Syria. Now, in the last months of 630, he organized an immense army—said to be 30,000 men—for an expedition to a town called Tabuk near the Gulf of Akaba. Evidently he did not plan a war of conquest, but only a show of strength to impress the tribes along the road to Syria. The tribes and settled communities of Jews and Christians saw the military and political power coming from Arabia, and decided that submission would be a wise course. By putting themselves peacefully under the protection of the Islamic state, they

A show of strength

would pay lighter taxes than if they resisted.

The march to Tabuk brought a new focus on the idea of *jihad*. For the first time, Muhammad had trouble gathering an army. Some men, tired of fighting, said they wanted to stay home. Meanwhile, the Prophet heard whispers of conspiracies. Muhammad felt that his mission to spread Islam required the loyal support of all Muslims. If the Islamic community was to grow, the energies of the Arabs—who could no longer carry on their traditional tribal raiding—would constantly have to be directed outward, toward new territories.

Muhammad insisted, therefore, that everyone should take part in his campaigns as a religious duty. He used persuasion and strict discipline to get the army on the road to Tabuk and to root out any disloyalty at home.

MUHAMMAD AT THE SUMMIT

In March 632, the Prophet led the *hajj*, or pilgrimage, to Mecca and announced the rituals to be observed. By including some of the traditional pagan practices, especially circumambulation of the Ka'ba, he emphasized the Arab roots of Islam. This helped make the new religion attractive to all the people of Arabia. The pilgrimage was now restricted to believers. From this time, only Muslims could worship at the Ka'ba.

Muhammad controlled only the region of Mecca and Medina, but he was probably the most powerful individual in Arabia and commanded the most wealth. More important, he had united the Arabs, town-dwellers and bedouins alike, in a

An old drawing of the Ka'ba shows the faithful circumambulating the shrine.

common religion—with a holy book of their own. They could take pride in their religion, believing it as true as any other, free of any foreign influence, and the ultimate revelation of God's will. The Arabs also had a growing sense of their own identity. The days of inter-tribal warfare were over. Now they were all part of one community, which offered stability, peace, and security—plus a spiritual motivation.

DEATH OF THE PROPHET

The "pilgrimage of farewell" was Muhammad's last public act. On returning to his home in Medina, he appeared to be growing weak. By June, apparently ill with a fever, he had to give up his activities—including plans for another expedition. On June 8, 632, Muhammad died peacefully. He was buried in his own house, which later became one of Islam's most treasured mosques.

Muhammad's funeral was marked by great emotion. One early follower reportededly threatened anyone who dared say that the Prophet was dead. Then Abu Bakr, as always the Prophet's right-hand man, spoke quietly: "O people, if anyone worships Muhammad, Muhammad is dead. But if anyone worships God, He is alive and dies not."

The mosque of Medina contains the Prophet's tomb.

CHAPTER SIX

MUHAMMAD THE MAN

Muhammad filled many roles in his vigorous life of sixty-two years—trader, merchant, visionary, prophet, leader, administrator, warrior, strategist, statesman. But what was he like as a person?

The Prophet was never regarded as divine. Although revered, he was not worshiped. He did not claim supernatural powers or anything that set him apart from ordinary humankind—except having been selected as God's Messenger. In short, Muslims believe that Muhammad was as human as all other men and women, with human needs and desires . . . and occasionally, in matters other than religion, small human faults.

Folklore and legends have attributed magical or supernatural abilities to Muhammad. Neither the Koran, however, nor the reliable historical biographies of the Prophet present him as anything other than a mortal man.

As for his appearance, detailed descriptions

of the Prophet have been preserved—but only in writing. Islamic tradition forbids pictures of Muhammad's face, to discourage believers from worshiping the Prophet along with God. Yet some people who knew him wrote descriptions, and these may give a fairly accurate idea of what he looked like.

Sturdy and of average height, Muhammad had dark hair, large black eyes, and a light complexion. His beard was thick, his forehead prominent, and his nose large. He walked so rapidly, it is said, that people had to hurry to keep up. Although the Prophet had a pleasant smile, he was not openly emotional. Often he appeared thoughtful and even sad. When he talked, he made his point, yet he was a master of tact and diplomacy. Constantly active, he planned his time well.

On occasion—for instance, when he felt danger from enemies' plotting—the Prophet dealt with his opponents severely. Straightforward opposition he respected, but he hated mockery and ridicule. He was especially sensitive to the jibes of hostile poets, and at times reacted with fierce anger and took drastic measures.

Muhammad was remembered more, however, for his sympathetic, kind, and gentle nature. He treated his followers with courtesy and respect. Children, too, were drawn to him, and he loved playing with them. A story is told of his comforting a little boy when the child's pet nightingale died. Muhammad seems to have felt a kindness toward animals that was unusual for the times. On the march to Mecca, it is said, the army passed a female dog that had just given birth. Muhammad posted a guard over the dog and puppies so that they would not be disturbed.

MUHAMMAD'S FAMILY

For a man who loved children, Muhammad may have been sad that he did not have more of his own . . . and especially sons. The two boys born to his first wife Khadijah died as infants. At the age of sixty, he again became the father of a boy, born to his Egyptian concubine, Mariyah. This brought him great joy—but not for long, because the child lived less than two years. His four daughters by Khadijah appear to have been his only offspring to reach adulthood, and they gave him grandchildren.

In the past, when Europeans criticized the Prophet, they often attacked his domestic life. He had, in fact, several wives. While married to Khadijah, Muhammad lived with her alone, in happiness. All his life he remembered her with admiration. After her death, he married other women. These marriage contracts were mainly for social, political, and economic reasons. Several were made to strengthen relationships with

Women were honored as wives and mothers and treated with respect.

important people—for example, Muhammad's marriage to 'Aishah, the daughter of Abu Bakr.

Another example was his marriage to the daughter of the Meccan leader Abu Sufyan— Muhammad's old enemy in the Battles of Badr,

Uhud, and Medina! Despite her father's opposition, she became a Muslim. Muhammad married her about 627, after the death of her husband. This union led to a reconciliation between Muhammad and Abu Sufyan and enabled Abu Sufyan to make peace between Muhammad and the Quraysh. Other marriages were intended to create good relations with defeated tribes.

In some instances, Muhammad married widows, who, according to the custom of the time, needed a man to provide for and protect them. Besides his wives, the Prophet had a few concubines—who could have the status of wife if they became Muslims. Mariyah, a gift from the ruler of Egypt, was a Christian and chose to keep her religion. Although she remained a concubine, she was treated as a wife after the birth of her son.

Besides these political, diplomatic, and charitable reasons, it seems clear that Muhammad enjoyed women's company. In his time and place, a powerful man often had several wives, for political alliances and personal pleasure. This was accepted practice.

'AISHAH

Each wife had her own room or small suite of rooms in the Prophet's house, which was probably enlarged a number of times. After Khadijah, his favorite wife was 'Aishah, daughter of Abu Bakr.

This remarkable young woman played a political role many years after the Prophet's death. She married the Prophet when still a child, but quickly showed herself to be intelligent and assured. With her charm and pretty looks, she apparently could say almost anything to her husband. Much of the information about Muhammad's private life comes from 'Aishah's recorded observations

Once a serious dispute broke out among the wives. Some were demanding a larger share of the property gained through warfare. According to tribal custom, Muhammad received a specific share of all spoils of war. He took only one-fifth instead of the customary one-fourth due a chief—and he gave most of his share to the poor. Fearing the effects of too much luxury, he insisted on a frugal life for his household. But when goods started coming in from military campaigns, his wives wanted more.

Muhammad grew so displeased over his wives' behavior that he withdrew from all of them for about a month. This threw the whole Muslim community into a panic. Marriage was an essential part of Arab society, and the Prophet's marriages represented not only political alliances but social stability. Finally, he offered each of his wives a choice between divorce and an agreement to live peaceably on his terms. Most, but evidently not

The site of Nebi Musa, a Muslim shrine, is believed to be the burial place of 'Aishah.

all, chose to stay, and the household became peaceful again.

The Koran states that the Prophet's wives could not remarry after his death. This seems unfair, but there was a reason behind it. If these women, with their prestige as wives of the Prophet, had remarried, they could have started new dynasties. A number of important families with rival claims of ties to the Prophet might weaken the Islamic community. Indeed, later history showed that this could happen.

MUHAMMAD'S VIEWS ON WOMEN

Muslim historians tend to emphasize the dreadful conditions of women's lives before Islam. The truth may be more moderate; we have the example of Khadijah, who ran her own business. Nonetheless, Islam did have a significant effect on women and certainly made changes for the better.

On the one hand, the Koran says that women are inferior to men in status and should obey them. It is men's duty to look after women, to provide for them, rule them, enjoy them, and in general, treat them fairly and kindly. Statements attributed to Muhammad repeat these ideas.

At the same time, the Koran states clearly that women and men are equal in religion: they are of equal value before God. The Koran emphasizes the importance of education and does not distinguish between men and women in this respect. It also sets down the specific rights due women. For instance, women have the right to inherit and own property and to bear witness in court, although not on an equal basis with men. While women are not allowed to ask for divorce, at

Women and men are of equal value

least they are allowed, if divorced, to keep the goods they received on their marriage. The rights granted women under Islam, though still limited, were an improvement over earlier conditions—and in some cases more than American women were allowed as recently as 150 years ago!

The question of multiple wives has always aroused debate. The Koran is usually interpreted to say that a man may have as many as four wives at one time. In a society where many men were killed in battle, this made it easier for widows to remarry and have the protection provided by a husband. But there is more to the koranic verse. It states that a man with two or more wives must treat each wife equally—and if he cannot, then he should have only one. It is clearly impossible to treat two or more individuals with absolute equality. Thus the Koran can be understood actually to favor one-wife marriage.

With his admiration for women and his vision of a good society, Muhammad tried to raise the status of women and ensure better treatment for them. After his death, however, more conservative rulers came to power. Under their rule, religious leaders made strict interpretations of the Koran and the *hadith*, and tightened the controls over women. Unfortunately, the relatively enlightened attitude that Muhammad showed appears to have been stifled by later religious leaders.

CHAPTER SEVEN

THE MESSAGE

In this account of the Prophet's life, we have learned something about what he preached. Now let us look more closely at that message, keeping in mind that Muhammad was not seeking to start a "new" religion but to restore the monotheistic faith established by Abraham.

ONE GOD

The essence of Muhammad's message is the belief in one God, Allah, the God of the Judaic and Christian religions. This requires the rejection of all other gods, deities, and idols. But what, according to the Koran, *is* God?

God is the creator of the universe and everything in it—not only the original creation but the ongoing process of life. God is the provider of all good things in life and has power over everything. An eternal presence, without beginning or end,

God exists everywhere, knows everything, and determines everything.

Adore your Lord who created you, as He did those before you, that you could take heed for yourselves and fear Him who made the earth a bed for you, the sky a canopy, and sends forth rain from the skies that fruits may grow—your food and sustenance. (Sura 2, verses 21–22)

Creator of the heavens and the earth from nothingness, He has only to say when He wills a thing: "Be," and it is. (Sura 2, verse 117)

If all the trees of the earth were pens and the oceans ink . . . the colloquy [words] of God would never come to an end. He is indeed all-mighty and all-wise. (Sura 31, verse 27)

The nature of God is merciful, benevolent, and compassionate. Loving humanity, God does not ask too much of individuals and forgives people their sins if they show repentance.

God does not burden a soul beyond [its] capacity. (Sura 2, verse 286)

Yet God is also capable of great anger and imposes harsh punishment for disbelief and wrongdoing. The verses of the Koran repeat these themes constantly: God's mercy and God's wrath.

> *Your Lord has prescribed grace for Himself, so that in case one of you commits evil out of ignorance, then feels repentant and reforms, He may be forgiving and kind.* (Sura 6, verse 54)
>
> *As for those who deny the signs of God, the punishment is severe.* (Sura 3, verse 4)
>
> *Do not destroy yourselves* [kill one another]. . . . *If someone does so through oppression or injustice, We shall cast him into Hell. This is how the Law of God works inevitably.* (Sura 4, verses 29-30)
>
> *The Lord said: "I punish only those whom I will, but My mercy enfolds everything."* (Sura 7, verse 156)

People may choose to accept or reject belief in God. Accepting Islam, a person must acknowledge God's goodness and show gratitude through daily prayer.

RIGHTEOUS LIVING

Gratitude toward God is also expressed by good behavior toward others and by living in the right way. The Koran sets forth rules for righteous liv-

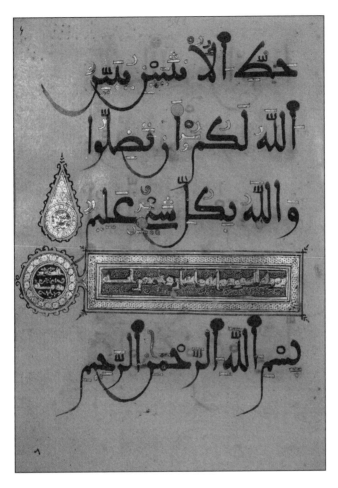

Manuscripts of the Koran are traditionally written in beautiful calligraphy and decorated with plant and geometric designs. This page is from a thirteenth-century Koran.

ing. People should live simply, taking care neither to be stingy nor to squander wealth. Too much love of wealth is a serious sin. People must be modest, avoid overweening pride, and not boast about their good deeds. Always, everyone should be kind, fair, and helpful to the needy.

> *Be good to your parents and relatives, the orphans and the needy, and the neighbors who are your relatives, and the neighbors who are strangers, and the friend by your side, the traveler, and your servants and subordinates.* (Sura 4, verse 36)
>
> *Saying a word that is kind and forgiving is better than charity that hurts. . . . Do not nullify your charity by . . . flaunting your favors like a man who spends of his wealth only to show off. . . .* (Sura 2, verses 263–264)
>
> *Be moderate in your bearing, and keep your voice low. Surely the most repulsive voice is the donkey's.* (Sura 31, verse 19)

Rulers, too, must strive for social justice. "The straight path," for rulers and ordinary people alike, is a frequent image in the Koran.

A Muslim should, like God, be compassionate and try to forgive others' mistakes and offenses. For example, the Koran offered alternatives to limit the violence of the blood feud, and Muhammad urged people to pardon those who did wrong. The believer also responds to God by engaging in *jihad.* "Holy struggle" has been interpreted to mean continuing effort to make the world accept the will of God and create a just society, along with the internal effort by each person to be virtuous.

The Koran says that human beings will always have to fight temptation—personified by the fallen angel, Satan. People must therefore use self-discipline, both moral and physical. They must avoid alcohol, certain foods, and gambling, which are harmful to the self. They must avoid actions that are harmful to others, including such

Muslims wash their hands at a special
fountain before entering a mosque for worship.

practices as usury (charging high interest on loans). But Islam is not ascetic (denying all pleasure), as was the faith of many early Christians. Muhammad enjoyed life and felt that all believers are entitled to a comfortable life and to warm human relationships.

REWARDS AND PUNISHMENTS

Most importantly, the virtuous Muslim will live in peace with God. He or she can also expect to enjoy a reasonable degree of prosperity. On the other hand, calamity—including natural disasters such as flood—can be a sign of God's displeasure with people who have been guilty of disobedience.

In Muslim belief, after death a person's soul survives in a way similar to that in Judaic and Christian beliefs. For the pagan Arabs this was a new concept, which they found hard to accept at first. A major part of Muhammad's message spoke of the afterlife and the Last Judgment.

We shall fix the scales of justice on the Day of Resurrection, so that none will be wronged in the least; and even if it [an action or deed] *were equal to a mustard seed in weight, we shall take it into account.* (Sura 21, verse 47)

On the Day of Judgment, whenever God determines it to happen, all souls will rise from their graves and be judged by God on the basis of their good and bad deeds during life. Righteous people will go to Paradise, where they will feel close to God and enjoy life everlasting in a beautiful, well-watered garden.

Surely the believers [Muslims] and the Jews and the followers of Christ . . . whoever believes in God and the Last Day, and whoever does right, shall have his reward with his Lord and will have neither fear nor regret. (Sura 2, verse 62)

Hell is the fate for the unrighteous and for nonbelievers, both those pagans who lived before the coming of Muhammad's message and those who rejected it. The Koran states that people guilty of such crimes as murder, failure to help the poor, corruption, and selfishness are also destined for hell, where they will suffer eternal fire.

THE PROPHET'S ROLE

The Koran often refers to biblical material, from both the Old Testament and the story of Jesus.

Remember We gave Moses the Book and sent after him many an apostle [messenger]; *and to Jesus, son of Mary, We gave clear evidence of the truth, reinforcing him with divine grace.* (Sura 2, verse 87)

The Koran does not say that human beings are born in sin and must be saved spiritually. Therefore, no savior or messiah is needed. Neither is any intermediary, such as a priest, needed between the individual and God. Most other religions, especially in the past, have priesthoods to mediate between ordinary human beings and the divine—but not Islam.

Nonetheless, Muslims must accept Muhammad's special role as the ultimate messenger of God. Muhammad brought the word of God to the people; exhorting, advising, and warning them, while revealing the rules by which they should live.

Islam regards all peoples as basically equal. That is, there are no superior or inferior races, tribes, or nations. If they are good Muslims, all individuals are equal in their religious merit. God values men and women, the slave and the master, equally. But in practical, nonreligious ways, inequalities do exist. Men are superior to women, the free man is above the slave, and the believer in Islam is superior to the nonbeliever.

THE FIVE PILLARS

The basic creed and actions that all Muslims must observe are called the "Five Pillars of Islam." First and most fundamental is belief in the unique God, with Muhammad as God's messenger. Second, every Muslim must pray five times a day, to focus his or her mind on God. The third Pillar, the giving of alms to the needy, reminds Muslims of generosity—always a central part of Muhammad's message of social reform and justice.

Fourth, Muslims must observe a complete fast from dawn to twilight for the month of Ramadan each year. The purpose of the fast is, again, to focus thoughts on God and how one can live according to God's wishes. It also encourages well-off people to be kinder to those who never have enough to eat. Finally, to strengthen faith, each Muslim must make the pilgrimage to Mecca at least once in his or her lifetime, if possible.

To sum up, in seventh-century Arabia—as today—Islam provided clear religious ideas and gave rules for worship and behavior in everyday life. More comprehensive and spiritually satisfying than paganism, the Islamic belief system appealed to people. In a remarkably short time, almost all of Arabia had accepted the Prophet's message. And that was just the beginning.

An old drawing shows the celebration of the end of Ramadan, a month of fasting.

CHAPTER EIGHT

THE YEARS AFTER MUHAMMAD'S DEATH

History tells of great empires that grew on one person's strength—only to crumble after that person's death. After the death of the Prophet, what would happen to the religion and the Islamic state that he founded?

Muhammad had no living sons, thus no heir to inherit his role as leader of the Islamic community. Nor had he named a successor. At his death, his followers must have not only faced grief but also confusion and worry. Anything could now happen to the small Islamic state. Factions could divide the community, rivals might sow trouble, enemies could attack, believers might fall away.

THE FIRST CALIPHS

For a few days, tension mounted as people argued over who should take Muhammad's place. But so committed to Islam were the Prophet's Companions, and so impressed were they by Abu Bakr's behavior during those troubled days, that a decision was made soon. Abu Bakr would be the first *caliph,* or successor—the religious and political leader of the Islamic state.

Although Abu Bakr led the community through the period after the Prophet's death, he lived for only two more years. He was followed by

The Muslim Empire to 750

Umar, another of the Prophet's Companions. While Umar's ten-year caliphate, or reign, was marked by his honesty and piety, he decreed harsher measures for women and non-Muslims. The next caliph was Uthman, who ordered the compiling of the revelations into the Koran. His rule was lax, however, and when strife developed, he was assassinated.

Next came 'Ali, the Prophet's cousin who had accepted Islam when Muhammad was starting his mission. 'Ali, brave and devout, married Muhammad's daughter Fatima. As caliph he tried to restore strict observance of Islamic principles and to rule with justice, but after five years, in 661, he was killed in battle.

An interesting sidelight concerns 'Aishah, the Prophet's wife. When Muhammad was alive, she had been the subject of a scandal and 'Ali had spoken of her unkindly. 'Aishah never forgave him, and in 656, the year 'Ali became caliph, she found her chance for revenge. She led a force against him near the Iraqi city of Basra, directing the battle from her camel—which inspired the name "Battle of the Camel." Although defeated, 'Aishah was allowed to spend the rest of her life peacefully in Medina.

The caliphate of 'Ali led to a permanent split in the Muslim world. Some Muslims believed that 'Ali was the only legal heir to Muhammad because of his family ties, and that only his descendants should hold the caliphate. After his death they broke from the main body of Islam and formed the *shiat 'Ali*, the "party of 'Ali." These are the Shi'ite Muslims, one of the two main sects within Islam today. They are dominant in Iran and numerous in Iraq, Syria, and Lebanon. The other main sect, which accepts the legality of the other caliphs, is called Sunni Islam, meaning "standard" or orthodox in beliefs and practices.

UMAYYAD AND ABBASID DYNASTIES

At 'Ali's death, the caliphate was taken over by a clan from Mecca. These caliphs, the Umayyads, moved the political capital from Medina to Damascus, although Mecca and Medina remained the religious center of Islam—as they are today. The Umayyads established a dynasty, with power passing from father to son, and ruled from 661 to 750. The Umayyads expanded Islam but imposed harsh measures on non-Arabs within the Islamic empire. They also indulged in luxurious living—a contrast to the simplicity preached by Muhammad. Their caliphate ended violently in a struggle with another family, the Abbasids, who based their claim on descent from Muhammad's uncle, Abbas.

The Abbasids, a more tolerant dynasty, then

moved the political capital from Damascus to Baghdad, which became a city of learning and splendor. This caliphate lasted until 1258, when Mongol warriors from central Asia overran much of the Middle East and caused great destruction.

As this survey shows, the religious vision that Muhammad inspired soon was affected by competition for worldly power. The Muslim armies, too, that advanced through the Middle East and North Africa, were motivated not only by religious zeal but by the riches of conquest.

Yet Islam would not have expanded so rapidly if its ideas and the Prophet's inspiration had not been so strong. To the victorious Muslims, it seemed that God was on their side, and their confidence must have won new believers. In many places, the Muslim conquerors were welcomed because people were tired of the oppressive rule of the Byzantine and Persian empires. While the growth of the Islamic community was achieved in part by warfare, the lives of people in the Middle East and North Africa did not necessarily became worse. Indeed Muslim rule often brought stability, orderly government, justice, and prosperity.

THE "GOLDEN AGE" OF ISLAM

Once the years of expansion were over and all the lands from India to Spain had been brought under

Muslim rule, a brilliant civilization blossomed. It benefited from the contributions of several different cultures: Persian, Egyptian, Syrian, Iraqi, and North African, as well as Arabian.

The time from the eighth century until nearly the fourteenth is often called the "Golden Age" of Islam. In cities all over the Muslim world, learning flourished—in science, medicine, philosophy, literature, astronomy, mathematics, and history. Muslim scholars and writers made valuable advances in knowledge. Architects designed splendid monuments, and artisans produced exquisite work. At its height, Islamic civilization was a model of tolerance, allowing non-Muslims to live peaceably and prosper under Muslim rule. World culture owes a great deal to the Golden Age of Islam, and to the contributions of Muslim individuals of all centuries.

The Islamic belief in God has brought spiritual guidance to countless millions of people the world over and may be the fastest-growing of all religious faiths today. Although sometimes sadly misunderstood, and affected by the anxieties and discord of our times, Islam holds a high ideal for human beings' relationship with God and with other human beings.

And it started with the vision and faith of one extraordinary man in an Arabian town, nearly 1,400 years ago—Muhammad, the Praised One.

The crescent and star, symbols of Muslim faith

CHRONOLOGY

A.D. 570 probable year of Muhammad's birth in Mecca

595 Muhammad's marriage to Khadijah

610 Muhammad first receives revelations, becomes the Messenger of God

613 Muhammad starts to preach publicly

615 some of Muhammad's followers seek refuge in Abyssinia (now Ethiopia)

619 death of Khadijah and of Abu Talib, head of Muhammad's clan and his protector

620 Muhammad's first contacts with pilgrims from Yathrib

622 July, Muhammad and his followers depart from Mecca for Yathrib (soon to be called Medina); start of the *Hijrah;* the "Constitution of Medina," an agreement between Muhammad and the people of Medina

623 Muhammad starts to raid Meccan caravans and send expeditions to win bedouin tribes

624 start of the practice of praying in the direction of the Ka'ba at Mecca

	Muhammad starts to expel the large Jewish tribes from Medina
625	Battle of Uhud
627	Siege of Medina ("Battle of the Trench"); destruction of the third and last large Jewish tribe
628	attempted pilgrimage to Mecca and resulting Treaty of Hudaybiya; conquest of oasis of Khaybar
629	Muhammad and followers make the pilgrimage
630	Muhammad and his army return in triumph to Mecca
	Battle of Hunayn
	Persian Empire weakens, South Arabian states turn to Muhammad
	Expedition to Tabuk
632	Muhammad leads the pilgrimage to Mecca, his last pilgrimage
	Muhammad dies at home, in June
	selection of Abu-Bakr as first caliph, or successor

GLOSSARY

Allah—the Arabic word for God, meaning the God of the Judaic, Christian, and Islamic faiths

bedouin—(Arabic) an Arab nomad, desert-dweller without a fixed home

blood-guilt, blood feud—in tribal custom, the revenge killing of a member of the tribe who committed murder. Continued revenge killing can lead to a blood feud between tribes.

caliph—(Arabic) successor; spiritual and political head of the Islamic community

circumambulation—the religious ritual of walking around a shrine

clan—several households descended from a common ancestor; part of a tribe

Companion—one of Muhammad's early followers who remained close to him all his life

convert—a person who has changed (converted) to a different faith

covenant—a binding agreement between two or more persons or groups

hadith—(Arabic) reports of the Prophet's sayings and actions

hijrah—(Arabic) emigration; specifically, the departure of the Muslims of Mecca for Medina in the summer of 622

Islam—the religion based on belief in one all-powerful God and submission to God's will according to the Koran and the teaching of the Prophet Muhammad. A Muslim is a follower of this religion.

jihad—(Arabic) "holy struggle" to defend and advance Islam and to live by Islamic principles

Ka'ba—the square stone building that was the main shrine in pagan Mecca and became the most sacred site in Islam

Koran—the holy book of Islam, consisting of revelations that Muslims believe were delivered from God to Muhammad

monotheism—religion based on belief in one deity

mosque—an Islamic house of worship

muezzin—(Arabic) a crier who calls Muslims to prayer five times in every 24 hours

nomads—people who move from place to place with their animal herds

pagan—referring to belief in multiple gods; a religion other than Judaism, Christianity, and Islam; a follower of pagan religion

pilgrimage—a visit, usually involving a journey, to a religious site such as a shrine

polytheism—belief in multiple deities

prophet—one who foretells the future and warns people of the consequences of their behavior

revelations—messages consisting of truths and warnings, often believed to have divine origin

Satan—the personification, or symbol, of evil. In Judaic, Christian, and Islamic belief, Satan was an angel who opposed God and was banished from heaven.

Shi'ite—one of the two main sects in Islam, based on the belief that 'Ali was the only rightful successor of the Prophet, along with certain other doctrinal beliefs different from those of the other main body of Islam (Sunnism)

shrine—a place designated for devotion to a saint or worship of a deity

Sunni—the "mainstream" sect of Islam, which accepts the first four successors of the Prophet

tribe—a large group believed to be descended from a common ancestor, made up of several clans

umma—(Arabic) the early community of Muslims

A NOTE ON SOURCES

The most helpful book I found in preparing to write this biography was W. Montgomery Watt's *Muhammad: Prophet and Statesman* (London: Oxford University Press, 1961). This is a well-balanced, readable condensation of his two earlier works, *Muhammad at Mecca* and *Muhammad at Medina*, which are recommended for a reader seeking more detailed information. Another useful and readable source was *Muhammad: A Biography of the Prophet* by Karen Armstrong (San Francisco: HarperSanFrancisco, 1992). Maxime Rodinson's book, *Mohammed* (London: Penguin Books, 1991; first published in French, 1961) offers a sympathetic and interesting, although somewhat controversial, interpretation of the Prophet. For more traditional accounts, I used Muhammad Husayn Haykal's *The Life of Muhammad,* eighth ed. (Indianapolis: North American Trust Publications, 1976); Martin Lings' *Muhammad, His Life Based on the Earliest Sources* (London: George Allen & Unwin, 1983); and A. Guillaume's translation of Ibn Hisham's abridgement of *The Life of Muhammad* by Ibn Ishaq

(Lahore: Oxford University Press, Pakistani Branch, 1955), the earliest known account of the Prophet's life.

Other works include Alfred Guillaume's *Islam* (London: Penguin Books, 1954); 'Ali Dashti's *Twenty Three Years: A Study of the Prophetic Career of Mohammad* (London: George Allen & Unwin, 1985); Tor Andrae's *Mohammed: The Man and His Faith* (New York: Harper & Bros., 1957); William E. Phipps' *Muhammad and Jesus: A Comparison of the Prophets and Their Teachings* (New York: Continuum Publishing Company, 1996); Michael Cook's *Muhammad* (Oxford: Oxford University Press, 1983) and H.A.R. Gibb's classic work, *Mohammedism,* eighth ed. (Oxford: Oxford University Press, 1970). As a general reference, I used *The Concise Encyclopedia of Islam* by Cyril Glasse (HarperSanFrancisco, 1991).

FOR MORE INFORMATION

BOOKS

Armstrong, Karen. *Islam: A Short History*. New York: Modern Library, 2000.

George, Linda S. *The Golden Age of Islam* New York: Marshall Cavendish, 1998.

Gordon, Matthew S. *Islam: World Religions*. New York: Facts on File, 1991.

Kelen, Betty. *Muhammad: The Messenger of God*. Nashville: Thomas Nelson, 1975.

Lippman, Thomas W. *Understanding Islam: An Introduction to the Moslem World*. New York: New American Library, 1982.

Pike, E. Royston. *Mohammed: Founder of the Religion of Islam*. New York: Roy, 1962.

Warner, Ruth. *Muhammad, Prophet of Islam*. New York: Franklin Watts, 1965.

The nineteenth-century writer Washington Irving wrote a surprisingly perceptive and fair-minded account of Muhammad's life: *Mahomet and His Suc-*

cessors. London: George Bell, 1909; first published in 1849.

An additional resource is the bimonthly publication *Saudi Aramco World,* which features illustrated articles on aspects of Islamic and Middle Eastern culture, history, and science. A free subscription may be requested from *Saudi Aramco World,* Box 469008, Escondido, CA 92046-9008.

INTERNET SITES

http://www.dnai.com/~gui/awairproductinfo.html
The website for Arab World and Islamic Resources and School Services (AWAIR).

http://www.islamicedfoundation.com/
Islamic Education Foundation (IFNA).

http://www.isna.net
The website of the Islamic Society of North America.

http://users.erols.com/zenithco/muhammad.html
Biographical information about Muhammad, with links to information about Islamic civilization and contributions to humanity

INDEX

ABOUT THE AUTHOR

Elsa Marston is a writer with a lifelong interest in the Middle East. She earned a degree in international affairs from Harvard University and, as the wife of a professor and writer from Lebanon, has lived in several countries of the Middle East and North Africa, with frequent sojourns in Beirut.

Ms. Marston's interest in the Arab–Islamic world has lead her to specialize in writing for young readers about the people of this region, past and present. Among her recent books are a novel, *The Cliffs of Cairo,* and several works of nonfiction: *Women of the Middle East: Tradition and Change* (co-authored with her son, Ramsay Harik); *The Ancient Egyptians; Lebanon: New Light in an Ancient Land;* and *The Phoenicians.* Her stories and articles appear in *Cricket* and *Highlights for Children.* "The Olive Tree," set in Lebanon, won the International Reading Association short story award in 1994. Ms. Marston dedicates this book to all people, of whatever faith, who respect the religions of others and work for a more peaceful world.